D0553667

MYSTICISM

THE EXPERIENCE OF THE DIVINE

MEDIEVAL WISDOM

CHRONICLE BOOKS

SAN FRANCISCO

A Labyrinth Book

First published in the United States in 1994 by Chronicle Books.

Copyright © 1994 by Labyrinth Publishing (UK) Ltd.

Design by Meringue Management

All rights reserved. No part of this book may be reproduced without written permission from the Publisher.

The Little Wisdom Library–Medieval Wisdom was produced by Labyrinth Publishing (UK) Ltd. Printed and bound in Italy.

Library of Congress Cataloging-in-Publication Data: Mysticism, Medieval Wisdom.

ISBN 0–8118–0484–4

1. Mysticism—History—Middle Ages, 600–1500. I. Chronicle Books (Firm) II. Series.

BV5075. M87   1994

248. 2' 2' 0902 — dc20   93–31709

CIP

Distributed in Canada by Raincoast Books,

112 East Third Avenue, Vancouver, B.C. V5T 1C8

10 9 8 7 6 5 4 3 2 1

Chronicle Books

275 Fifth Street, San Francisco, CA 94103

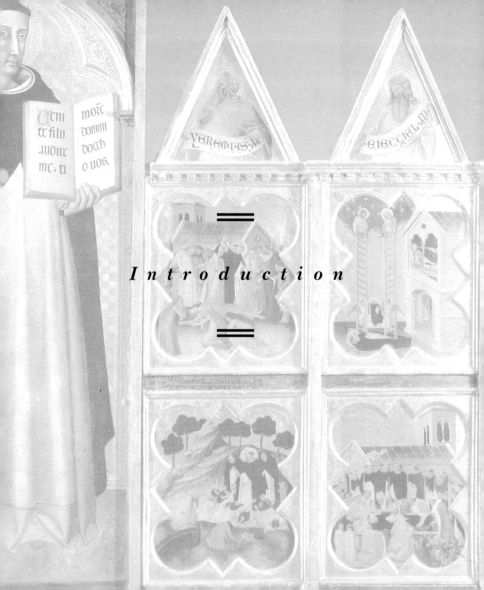

Introduction

The art and practice of contemplation has been a characteristic element in Christianity since its inception, although it has never been unique to the Christian religions. In Eastern religions, it tended to take a depersonalized form in which the self was unified with the divine being. Whereas in the Christian West, the idea of Augustine of Hippo that the basis of understanding was the love of God made the mystical experience primarily a relationship between persons, a progressively deepening psycho-

logical journey which brought the pilgrim finally to contemplate the very essence of God. In the monastic solitude sought by great numbers of Christians in the early centuries, Christian mysticism took shape as the highest form of spiritual life. It was a vocation universally respected, since holy men and women were seen as powerful advocates for their sinful fellows before the court of heaven.

Another enduring feature of mysticism in the Christian West was its accessibility. Since love and not understanding was its starting point, anybody could embark on the path of spiritual learning. At first, it was taken for granted that it would involve living like a hermit or monk. Later, after Richard of St. Victor in the twelfth century and Bonaventure in the thirteenth had focused the object of contemplation on the Incarnation and Passion of Christ, its practice was broadened to include the less rigorous circumstances of nuns and anchoresses and, increasingly, the laity. In the fourteenth century, spiritual directors (who were usually educated Dominican or Franciscan friars, but who wrote

increasingly in the vernacular) were beginning to stimulate an intense spirituality in a widening sector of the laity. As time passed, this new spirituality took on various forms and gained many adepts outside the narrow monastic world.

Many of the disciples of teachers like Meister Eckhart and Henry Suso in the Rhineland, or Richard Rolle and Walter Hilton in England, were women. Some of them wrote accounts of their religious experiences, which were frequently expressed in the language of secular love poetry and were often works of profound psychological understanding: most notably, the *Spiritual Poems* of Hadewijch of Antwerp in Dutch, the *Dialogo* of Catherine of Siena in Italian, and the *Revelations of Divine Love* of Julian of Norwich in English. The flowering of mystical thought and experience among the fourteenth-century laity brought Western spirituality to new heights, which were only surpassed, if at all, by St. John of the Cross and St. Teresa of Avila.

Inevitably, the result of accessibility was that some devotees embraced eccentric and often unorthodox forms of spirituality, to their teachers' frequent chagrin. St. Francis, an obedient son of the Church, inspired the Fraticelli heretics, extremist proponents of absolute poverty. Others allowed their religious euphoria to suspend their conscience, believing that a direct line to God excused them from moral precepts: Amaury of Bene and the motley believers in the Free Spirit who took this line were probably representative of a much broader movement, which indeed reappeared in the Reformation and later. In general, as the practice of contemplation grew among the multiplying educated laity, the end of the Middle Ages

Opening pages: Two illuminations by Hildegarde of Bingen, 12th Century Rhineland mystic. *Pages 8–9:* A shrine to St. Dominic, founder of the Dominicans, noted for their role in bringing the concept of religious devotion into everyday life.

became a golden era of religious individuality.

In the Reformation period, both Protestant and Catholic authorities became suspicious of the contemplatives, and many, like Miguel de Molinos, were persecuted. But the art was passed on, immortalized in the printed texts of its greatest literature, and the contemplation theme reemerges in authors of all religious persuasions, from George Herbert in the seventeenth century to Simone Weil and Thomas Merton in our own: a striking achievement of medieval wisdom.

Jeremy Catto

Fellow, Oriel College, Oxford

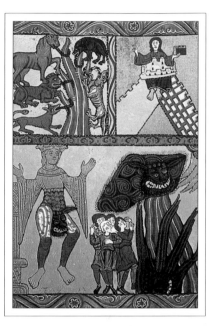

Pages 10–11: Panels of a stained glass window portraying the English mystic Julian of Norwich worshiping Christ. *Above:* Hildegarde's vision of the end of time.

The Perfection
of the Spirit

The mystic experience is most commonly defined as the experience of union with the divine or transcendent. As such, it is an individual and private phenomenon and does not have a fixed home in any one religious tradition, nor is it limited to any particular age. Mystics have appeared in all cultures, in all ages; they have flourished within the great organized religions as well as outside them. There have been Christian, Jewish and Muslim mystics as well as Hindu, Buddhist and Taoist ones. And there have been mystics who were simply themselves, part of no tradition and not even recognizing any entity that they would call "God." Thus to speak of "medieval mysticism" is an artifice, adopted here for the purpose of presenting just one slice of a human experience that spans the whole of human history, including the present day. It is a rich slice, however—religious life in the Middle Ages was characterized by a rare spirit of inquiry, controversy and experimentation. The Christian Church was just a few centuries old, still in the process of defining its doctrine, its organization, its rituals, and its understanding of the nature both of its God and the man Jesus who was its inspiration and founder. In this process of

Previous pages: Persian painting showing Sufi mystics conversing in a garden. *Right background:* Hildegarde's vision of God.

When the soul reaches the perfection of the

Spirit, being completely purified from passion,

and is joined and commingled with the

Holy Spirit ... then it becomes all light,

all exultation, all heartfelt love,

all goodness and lovingkindness.

Macarius, fourth century Coptic hermit

definition, the mystics of the Church played a profoundly influential, and sometimes controversial role.

From the earliest so-called Desert Fathers who took up solitary lives of asceticism and contemplation in the Syrian and Egyptian deserts in the first centuries following Jesus' crucifixion, to the sixteenth century when Teresa of Avila in Spain wrote that God was "present in all things," and "my life is the life which God has lived in me," the mystics of the Christian Church served as living examples of reli-

gious scripture. The circumstances of their lives, their descriptions of their experiences, and the conclusions they drew from these experiences about the nature of God and human life, were varied and sometimes contradictory. But the medieval mystics, like mystics of all ages, were possessed of a luminous and magnetic quality that attracted the respect and veneration of others around them, and so inevitably shaped the religious and spiritual aspirations of their age.

Above: Hildegarde portrays the Church as a "mother" figure, reflecting the light of God like the moon reflects the light of the sun. *Right:* Franciscan monks arrive in Flanders.

Mystics

of the

Desert

Paul the Simple, Isaac of the Cells, Macarius the Great, Simeon the Stylite, John the Dwarf—these were among the colorful names of mystics who were scattered across the deserts of Syria and Egypt in the early years of Christianity. Some of them traveled from village to village, gathering followers along the way. Some lived in caves or small huts, receiving the pilgrims who sought them out for spiritual advice. Others were wild and adamantly solitary, living without even clothing or shelter.

A group known as the Stylites retreated to live atop pillars built of stone, exposed to the elements and living only on what food and water was brought to them by their admirers. They became known as the Desert Fathers, and the totality of their commitment to the spiritual life strongly influenced the early Church.

St. Antony, perhaps one of the most well known of the Desert Fathers, is considered to be the true originator of Christian monastic life. Born of a wealthy Egyptian family in 251 A.D., he renounced his inheritance at the age of thirty and moved into a solitary hut in the desert near his native village. However, his charisma was such

Previous pages: Paulist monastery in Egypt.
Right background: Fresco on a wall of St. Antony's monastery in the Egyptian desert.

In the exercise of mystical contemplation

leave behind the senses and the activities

of the intellect, and all things sensible and intellectual

... that thou mayest arise, as far as thou mayest,

by unknowing, towards union with

Him who transcends all being and all knowledge.

Dionysius, *Mystical Theology*

that he soon began to be visited by seekers and admirers. He then walled himself up in a deserted fort for twenty years, emerging only to move even farther into the wilderness. But always he was surrounded by those seeking his counsel or his blessings. Finally, just before his death at the age of 100, Antony entrusted the care of those who had gathered around him to one of his chief disciples, Pachomius. And it was Pachomius, in the fourth century, who began to structure and organize these ascetics and seekers into monastic communities.

A touching story is told in the *Sayings of the Fathers*, compiled and

Above: Russian portrait of St. Antony. *Right:* "A Hermit at Prayer" by Gerrit Dou, 17th C.

published in the twelfth century, of an exchange typical of those between the mystics of the desert and those who gathered around them. The account concerns John the Dwarf and one of his elderly and absent-minded disciples. The older man would often consult John, and, as often, immediately forget what he had been told. Painfully aware of his own lapses in memory, the old man once approached his Master with an embarrassed apology. John the Dwarf reportedly said, "Go and light a lamp." The old man did as he was told. Then John said, "Bring some more lamps, and light them from the first." Again, the old man obeyed. John asked him, "Has that lamp suffered any loss from the fact that other lamps have been lit from it?" The old man said, "No." John said, "So it is with John;

even if the whole of Scetis came to see me, they would not separate me from the love of Christ. Consequently, whenever you want to, come to me without hesitation."

The cloisters and monastic orders of the later medieval period were both centers of spiritual life and centers of learning. It was here that Greek, Arabic, Persian, and Aramaic texts began to be translated into Latin, and were discussed in the noble courts with which these religious communities were affiliated. The cathedral schools and the universities both quickened the pace of translations of ancient texts and broadened the influence of their teachings. Among the teachings that made their way into religious debates and discussions, a set of writings attributed to Dionysius the Areopagite were particularly influential.

Dionysius was St. Paul's convert at Athens, and, as the alleged source of a collection of writings entitled *The Mystical Theology* and *The Divine Names*, he no doubt gave them an air of sanctity and weight they might not have enjoyed otherwise. Most scholars today think the treatises were actually written by a monk in Syria, probably around the sixth century, and the author has now come to be known as "Pseudo-Dionysius." They were first translated from

Right: Illumination from a manuscript about the life of St. Dominic.

Greek into Latin in the ninth century by an Irish theologian and philosopher, John Scotus Erigena. Erigena's own philosophy was profoundly influenced by the texts, and his elaborations on the treatises formed the basis of two religious movements condemned as heretical.

Union with the divine, says *The Mystical Theology,* is the goal of human life – and, it is implied, *this* life, not a life in the hereafter. In order to reach this state one must be free of all thought, emotion, and sensation. To dwell permanently in this deified state, furthermore, requires "the unceasing and absolute renunciation of ourselves and of all things." The central themes of these treatises are found in many of the teachings of the Desert

Fathers, and formed the theological basis of much of Christian mysticism in the Middle Ages.

The Influence
of Neo-Platonism

Not all of mysticism in medieval Europe was confined within the boundaries of the Christian Church, of course. Throughout the Middle Ages, the mysticism of the Neo-Platonists, particularly as expressed in the writings of Plotinus, remained a powerful influence on religious and philosophical thought. Though Plotinus himself was a pagan, the view of reality he expressed in his writings was one which corresponded to the experience of mystics,

Behold,

Thou wert within,

and I abroad.

St. Augustine, *Confessions*

regardless of their religious affiliation.

Plotinus was born in Egypt during the third century, educated in Alexandria and finally settled in Rome. His *Enneads,* comprised of six books of nine sections each, were his attempt not only to describe the mystical experience but to help others to experience it as well. The cosmology Plotinus constructed was based on Platonic ideas, and as his writings were introduced into the realm of medieval scholasticism, they

Previous pages: Portrait of St. Augustine, illustrating the manuscript, *De Civitate Dei.*
Right background: "All of creation is a symphony of joy and jubilation." — Hildegarde.

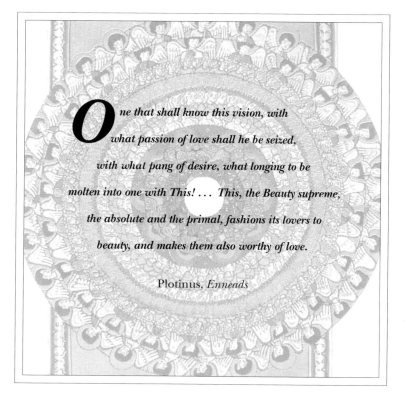

One that shall know this vision, with
what passion of love shall he be seized,
with what pang of desire, what longing to be
molten into one with This! ... This, the Beauty supreme,
the absolute and the primal, fashions its lovers to
beauty, and makes them also worthy of love.

Plotinus, *Enneads*

captured the imagination of theologians and philosophers in many ways, both straightforward and subliminal.

"The souls of men are not cut off from their origin," Plotinus insisted. "Though they have descended even to earth, yet their higher part holds for ever above the heavens." And in his view, the way to unity with the Absolute was most effectively by negation, *via negativa.* "Cut away everything" that is not the One, he said, and thereby reach an inner freedom and detachment from external things that leaves one "self-encentered, beholding a marvelous beauty, acquiring identity with the divine." This process he called "the flight of the alone to the Alone," and although the seeker can prepare for its happening, there is nothing one can do to grasp it. "In this seeing we neither hold an object [in the mind], nor trace distinction, nor are there two. The man is changed, no longer himself nor self-belonging; he is merged with the Supreme, sunken into it, one with it." In this

> While the soul is self-recollected and forgetful of all things, it is prepared for the inflowing and teaching of the Holy Spirit, who will withdraw himself from thoughts that lack understanding.
>
> St. John of the Cross, sixteenth century

description, Plotinus agrees with mystics of both East and West, through all ages and times.

The ideas of Plotinus and Neo-Platonism were brought into the Christian framework by Augustine, born in the fourth century in what is now Algeria of a pagan father and a Christian mother. At first attracted to Manichaeism, he discovered Neo-Platonism as a lecturer in Milan, largely through works of Plotinus that had recently been translated into Latin. It was during this time that he had the first of several "glimpses" of mystical experience, which he later described in his *Confessions*. His conversion to Christianity was undertaken after years of internal struggle between his mystic longings and the joys of married life, material advantage, and respectability. After it, he spent most of his life in North Africa where he served as bishop of Hippo and produced a vast body of written work that was to influence theologians and scholars for centuries to follow.

Clothe thyself

in the garment of

nothingness and

drink the cup of

self-annihilation.

Attar, 12th C.

Persian Sufi mystic

سماع صطافی بسیار میکردند و بدین با

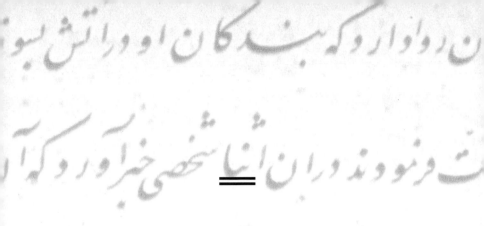

The Mysticism

of Devotion

The actual experience of the mystic contains no contradiction between what we would call "devotion" and what we would call "detachment." But the language mystics are forced to use is bound by distinctions and dualities—hence their continual insistence that words are inadequate. Unfortunately for the listeners, though, there is no way to comprehend just how inadequate the words are until they somehow stumble upon the mystical experience themselves.

A further confusion arises due to the different uses of particular words. Richard of Saint Victor, the twelfth century theologian of mysticism, attempts this definition: "Thinking roams about; meditation investigates; contemplation wonders." By meditation he, and most other Christian theologians, do not mean the state of thought-free receptivity that the word connotes in Eastern terms. Rather, meditation in Richard's terms is nearer to devotional prayer, a form of concentration where the seeker focuses his or her entire attention on God, or on Christ as God's human manifestation. To the Christian mystic, it is in a state of contemplation that the seeker finds the transcendent union with the divine known as meditation in the East.

Previous pages: Persian painting of Sufi dervishes.
Right background: "Caritas" (Love) by Hildegarde of Bingen.

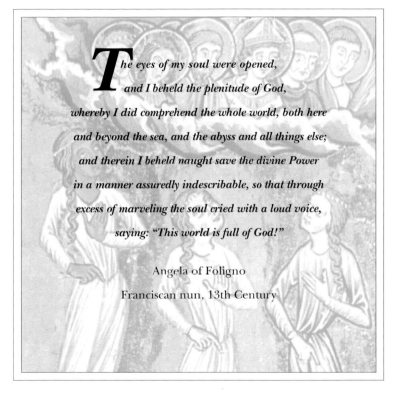

The eyes of my soul were opened,
and I beheld the plenitude of God,
whereby I did comprehend the whole world, both here
and beyond the sea, and the abyss and all things else;
and therein I beheld naught save the divine Power
in a manner assuredly indescribable, so that through
excess of marveling the soul cried with a loud voice,
saying: "This world is full of God!"

Angela of Foligno

Franciscan nun, 13th Century

Two of the Christian saints, Bernard of Clairvaux and Francis of Assisi, were probably the most well known of the devotional mystics. Bernard, who was a distinguished Cistercian and was instrumental in founding the Templars, spoke often of the relation between God and the seeker as that between spiritual bridegroom and bride. The object of Francis' love was Jesus more than God Himself, but certainly to Francis there was no conflict between the two. In this love, Francis sought to become more and more like Jesus, until he finally even developed on his own body the same wounds Christ had suffered in the crucifixion.

Neither Bernard nor Francis were the type to confine themselves to lives of solitude and withdrawal from the world. Each, in their own way, combined activity with repose, good works in the world with work upon themselves. As Bernard once said, "Let works of piety accompany the labors of penitence which strengthen the soul... To the nourishment of good works let there be added...the draught of prayer."

The mystics of the devotional type generally describe their experience as one of "hearing the voice of God," as did Catherine of Siena, or as being gifted with elaborate visions, such as those of Hildegarde of Bingen or Rupert of Deutz. And when they return to their ordinary state from these ecstasies of mystic union, their pain is as great as the pain of lovers separated. In Christian mysticism, as in the Eastern traditions, these "dark nights of the soul" are seen as a necessary part of the mystic's growth towards a state of permanent union with the divine.

The Book of the Lover and the Beloved

One of the more intriguing books from the Middle Ages reflecting the devotional stream in Christian mysticism is attributed to Ramon Lull, a Catalan of the thirteenth century who was a Franciscan tertiary, or lay member of the order of St. Francis. This same person has also been described as a hermetic doctor and an alchemist, and it is likely that Lull was one of those charismatic medieval figures whose name was placed on manuscripts by other authors in order to give them greater validity and appeal.

The Book of the Lover and the Beloved tells a tale that captures the more romantic and freewheeling spectrum of medieval mysticism. In it, Lull tells the story of his own renunciation of a decadent courtly life, provoked by an encounter with a married noblewoman he had been shamelessly pursuing for some time. Finally, in consultation with her husband, the woman arranged to meet Ramon in a secluded place. He arrived expecting that he was at last about to gain her favors, but instead she pulled aside her dress to reveal a suppurating breast cancer. "See, Ramon," the woman commanded, "the foulness of this body that has won thy affection! How much better hadst thou done to have set thy love on Jesus Christ, of Whom thou mayest have a prize that is eternal!"

Shocked to the core, Ramon renounced all worldly desires, and among the legends told about him are that he traveled to North Africa to engage in public debates with Muslims, and there "convert or be converted." His contact with Muslims, is also mentioned in the preface to his book, where his fictional character Blanquerna decides to "make a book of the Lover and the Beloved, in which Lover should be a faithful and devout Christian and the Beloved should be God."

Lull's character has, he tells us, once been a Pope. At that time, he had heard from one of the Saracens that they "have certain

Page 38: Statue of Catherine of Siena. *Right background:* Hildegarde's self portrait.

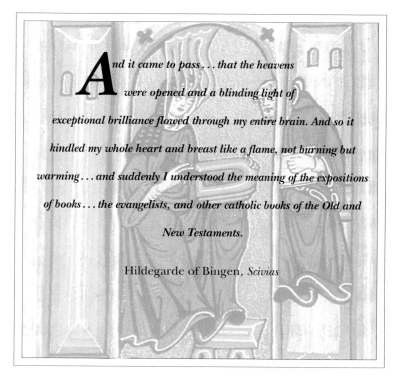

And it came to pass . . . that the heavens were opened and a blinding light of exceptional brilliance flowed through my entire brain. And so it kindled my whole heart and breast like a flame, not burning but warming . . . and suddenly I understood the meaning of the expositions of books . . . the evangelists, and other catholic books of the Old and New Testaments.

Hildegarde of Bingen, *Scivias*

The Lover was all alone, in the shade of a fair tree.

Men passed by that place, and asked him why he was alone.

And the Lover answered: I am alone, now that I have seen you

and heard you; until now, I was in the company of my Beloved.

...

The Lover and the Beloved met, and the Beloved said to the Lover:

Thou needest not to speak to Me. Sign to Me

only with thine eyes—for they are words to My heart—that I may give

thee that which thou doest ask of Me.

Ramon Lull, *The Book of the Lover and the Beloved*

religious men, and that among others are certain men called Sufis, who are the most prized among them, and these men have words of love and brief examples which give to men great devotion; and these are words which demand exposition and by the exposition thereof the understanding soars aloft and the will likewise soars and is increased in devotion."

The Book of the Lover and the Beloved was written in the vernacular, and as such was obviously intended for the laity. It consists of 366 short verses, one for every day of the year. The content of the verses points to the mystic union with

God through devotion, and the book remains one of the most charming and accessible written works of the medieval period.

Left background: Statue of Bernard of Clairveaux. *Right:* Portrayal of St. Francis receiving his stigmata.

Mystics of the Rhineland School

Of the medieval mystics whose experiences conformed to the inward realization commonly called "*via negativa*," or the way that emphasizes negation and detachment, Meister Eckhart stands out as one who devoted enormous energy to the task of transmitting the secrets of this path to others. Again, it is important to stress that Eckhart himself would not make this division between the negative and positive path, between the path of detachment and the path of love. He says, in fact, "Through knowledge I receive God into myself, and through love I enter into Him." The "knowledge" of which he speaks is not book-learning but the purification of the mind from accumulated impressions that interfere with the direct perception of reality. Thus emptied, God can enter in. By devoting oneself to the quest— "through love"—the seeker has made the step necessary to meet Him halfway.

Previous pages: Ivory carving in the Kunsthistoriches Museum, Vienna. *Above:* Hildegarde's "cosmic wheel." *Right background:* Hildegarde's vision of one of the demons that can plague the mystic.

> *God is such that we apprehend Him better by negation than by affirmation.*
>
> Meister Eckhart

Eckhart's efforts to communicate his experience earned him a good deal of trouble from Church authorities, and late in his life he found himself defending many of his statements during a trial before the Inquisition in Cologne. In examining the objections raised by the Inquisitors, and Eckhart's response to them, one is again reminded of the difficulties mystics faced in adapting ordinary language to descriptions of extraordinary truths. Eckhart was accused, for example, of saying that "there is something in the soul that is uncreated and uncreatable"—a statement that presumably was interpreted to be an affront to God's reputation. In fact, Eckhart points out, he had said, "There is something in the soul that is so akin to God that it is one with Him.... It has nothing in common with anything that is created." A subtle point, and one that was apparently lost on the authorities—numerous portions of Eckhart's published teachings were condemned by a Papal bull issued in Avignon in 1329.

As founder of "the Rhineland school," Eckhart had a profound influence on German mysticism in particular. While St. Francis was a renunciate of physical luxuries, Eckhart was a renunciate of all externally gathered ideas. "Man should not rest satisfied with an imaginary God," he said in one of his sermons. "When the thoughts pass away the God also disappears. But one should have an essential God, who is far above the thought of man and of all creatures."

As a preacher, Eckhart spoke in the vernacular and was intimately involved with the lives and concerns of the laity. His sermons implicitly attacked the long-held idea that a religious life was possible only within cloisters removed from the world. "One must learn an inner solitude, wherever one may be," he said, and

> The more she is empty of all things which are not God, the more purely she receives God, the more she is in God, and the more she becomes one with God. And she looks at God and God looks at her from face to face, as transformed into one image.
>
> Meister Eckhart, *The Book of Divine Consolations*

insisted that the true renunciation was not of kingdoms but of one's perception of oneself as an entity separate from God. Finally, and perhaps most "heretically" of all, Eckhart appeared to go against the teachings that insisted on following Jesus through imitation of his godly behavior, pointing instead to the divinity he believed everyone contained: "People never need to think so much about what they ought to do," he said, "but they should remember what they are." And, "It is more worthy of God that He should be born spiritually of every virgin, or of every good soul, than that He should have been born physically of Mary."

Many of Eckhart's disciples, after his condemnation by the Inquisition, were careful to distance themselves from their master, even though they might have continued to abide by his teachings. Others, like Henry Suso, Jan Ruysbroeck, John Tauler, and the authors of *Theologia Germanica* continued to openly identify themselves with Eckhart, and some time after his death they formed an association, including laymen, called the Friends of God.

> Earthly lovers, however greatly they may love, must needs bear to be distinct and separate from one another; but Thou, O unfathomable fullness of all love...in virtue of Thy being absolutely all in all, pourest Thyself so utterly into the soul's essence that no part of Thee remains outside.
>
> *The Life of Blessed Henry Suso by Himself*

The Mystic Heresies

Meditation, say the saints, is the seeking, discussing, ruminating and chewing of the divine food. And if this food is always ruminated, if it is perpetually chewed, it remains in the mouth and is never swallowed. Thus it cannot be quietly held and digested in the stomach and it brings no life or nourishment to a man.... Meditation is a means of reaching an end, and the end of meditation is contemplation. Contemplation is finding; it is the enjoyment and retention of the divine food in the stomach. It is the goal, the end of the road where a person understands and knows God.

Miguel de Molinos, *Defense of Contemplation*

Christ himself was one who spoke often and eloquently of union with the divine, but some of the mystics who appear to have shared his experience attracted the suspicion and sometimes outright enmity of the medieval Church. At the root of the suspicion was perhaps a sincere effort to prevent seekers from falling into one of the many pitfalls along the spiritual path, such as the delusions and hallucinations that could be mistaken for the genuine mystical experience. At the root of the enmity was no doubt the same fanaticism that engendered the Inquisition, and its authoritarian attempts to establish

Previous pages: A scene from the Inquisition by Goya. The persecution of heretics begun in the Middle Ages continued well into the 18th century. *Right:* Joan of Arc, burned as a heretic but later declared a saint by the Church.

the doctrines of the Christian Church as the only legitimate guide to religious experience. Along the way, more than a few unorthodox ideas earned their adherents dispossession of their wealth and reputation, long prison sentences, or even death.

The Amaurian Heresy of the Free Spirit

Two strong heretical movements with overtly mystical doctrines emerged in the thirteenth century, both directly antagonistic to the Church. The first was based on the philosophy of John Scotus Erigena, the translator of the Neo-Platonist "Dionysius" texts. Erigena's book, *On the Division of Nature,* was the basis of lectures given by Amaury of Bene at the University of Paris early in the thirteenth century.

In them, he spoke of a doctrine of the Free Spirit, and proclaimed that the entire Church, as it was presently constituted, was destined to pass away. In its place would emerge a new era in human spirituality based on the inner consciousness of God—and that consciousness, naturally, would need no organized priesthood or church.

Amaury was posthumously condemned as a heretic in 1210, and eleven of his disciples were burned at the stake. But the doctrine of the Free Spirit was an idea that would not die so easily, and it re-emerged later in the thirteenth century among men and women known as the Beghards and the Beguines. The Council of Vienne, in turn, condemned the heresy of the Free Spirit in 1312, but its popularity continued to spread, sometimes among the Friends of God who followed Eckhart's teachings. Most notable among them was Nicholas of Basle who was burned as a heretic in the late fourteenth century. Certainly, the Free Spirit teachings took Eckhart's views to an extreme that was more closely allied with the Tantric mysticism of the East than with any of the views of the mystics who had remained within the framework of Christian orthodoxy. The Bishop of Strasbourg noted that these heretics claimed that "the soul's inward voice is safer than the truths preached in the church" and that "nobody will be lost [in the end], not even Jews or Saracens, because their spirits will return to God."

The Eternal Gospel

Joachim of Fiore, who died in 1202, was not familiar with the Amaurian doctrines, which makes the commonality between his vision and that of the doctrine of the Free Spirit all the more intriguing. Both the Amaurians and the Eternal Gospel preached by Joachim and his followers asserted that there were three ages in the history of the world—that of the Father, the Son, and the Holy Spirit. Both groups characterized the ages of the Father and the Son as ages of servile obedience and fear, and filial subjection and faith, respectively. Both said that the age of the Holy Spirit was imminent, and would make the church obsolete. The main features of the age would be liberty, love, and contemplation. The world would become a vast monastery populated by human beings with "spiritual bodies" in unity with God, and the Eastern and Western churches would be reunited.

Many mystics of the later medieval period tread just this side of heresy during their lifetimes, including Teresa of Avila, Francis of Assisi, and John of the Cross. The authoritarian tendencies within the Church that resulted in the Inquisition did not tolerate individual mystics easily, and many were called to justify their experiences in rigorous examinations by their superiors. In their book, *The Common Experience*, authors J. M. Cohen and J.-F. Phipps argue that mystical teaching within the Roman Catholic Church came to an end, at least temporarily, with the seventeenth century trial of Miguel de Molinos.

"Thinking roams about; meditation investigates; contemplation wonders, Richard of Saint-

Victor had said. Molinos, in his popular book *Spiritual Guide*, addressed himself to the question of wonder, the point on the path where the mystic must take a step out of meditation, or devotional prayer, and into contemplation. There is a point in spiritual practice, Molinos argued, when it no longer profits the seeker to concentrate on God. "His inclination is to stay still, said Molinos of the meditator. His only pleasure is to remain calm and silent, calmly and lovingly aware that he is with God and attending only to Him."

Molinos himself was insistent that his views were entirely consistent with the teachings of Christ. Contemporary chroniclers of the trial reported that he was at all times gracious, composed and

Above: Religion igniting the heavenly fires; 15th C. Italian painting. *Right:* St. Francis and stories from his life, by Berlinghieri. *Following page:* Hildegarde's "egg of creation."

serene in presenting his views. In convicting Molinos on charges of heresy and condemning him to prison, where he spent nine years before he died, the Inquisitors of the Church implied that their concern  – perhaps arising from a natural tendency of the mind to attach itself to the familiar, the known, the rational. In fact it is a testimony to the openness of the medieval church that so many mystics managed to emerge was with preserving forms and rituals more than with the spiritual enlightenment of the individual. They were, in the words of Molinos, more interested in chewing the food than in swallowing and digesting it.

It is an attitude that can be found throughout the history of all ages, all cultures, all organized religions within it and survive. And it is a testimony to the divine within the human spirit that no matter how persecuted, ridiculed or constrained it may be, it emerges in all ages, in all cultures and religious settings, with a unity of experience that transcends the limitations of space and time.

BIBLIOGRAPHY

Attar. *The Persian Mystics.* M. Smith, trans. John Murray, London, 1932.

Bancroft, Anne. *The Luminous Vision: Six Medieval Mystics and Their Teachings.* Allen & Unwin, London, 1982.

Cohen, J. M. and J.-F. Phipps. *The Common Experience.* Rider & Co., London, 1979.

Meister Eckhart (2 vols.). J. Evans, trans. Watkins, London, 1924.

Julian of Norwich. *Revelations of Divine Love.* Metheun, London, 1901.

Lull, Ramon. *The Book of the Lover and the Beloved.* E. Allison Peers, trans. Society for Promoting Christian Knowledge, London, 1946.

Philokalia. *Writings from the Philokalia.* E. E. Kadloubovsky and G. E. H. Palmer, trans. Faber, London, 1951.

Plotinus. *The Enneads.* S. McKenna, trans. Faber, London, 1956.

Strong, Thomas. *Mystical Christianity.* Regency Press, London, 1978.

Suso, Henry. *The Little Book of Eternal Wisdom.* J. M. Clark, trans. Faber, London, 1953.

Teresa of Avila. *The Life of Santa Teresa.* J. M. Cohen, trans. Penguin, 1957.

Anselm. *The Prayers and Meditations of St. Anselm.* B. Ward, ed. London: Penguin Books, 1973.

Davies, O. *Meister Eckhart, Mystical Theologian.* London: SPCK, 1991.

Englebert, O. *St. Francis of Assisi.* Ann Arbor: Servant Publications, 1979.

Hildegard of Bingen. *Book of Divine Words.* M. Fox, ed. Santa Fe: Bear & Co. Inc., 1990.

Hilton, Walter. *The Ladder of Perfection.* L. Shirley-Price, ed. London: Penguin Books, 1988.

Julian of Norwich. *Revelations of Divine Love.* C. Wolters, ed. London: Penguin Books, 1952.

Leclercq, J. F. Vandenbroucke, and L. Bouyer. *The Spirituality of the Middle Ages.* Tunbridge Wells: Burns & Oates Ltd., 1968.

Thomas à Kempis. *Imitation of Christ, L.* Shirley Price, ed. London: Penguin Books, 1966.

Underhill, E. *Mysticism.* Oxford: Oneworld Publishing, 1993.

Every effort has been made to trace all present copyright holders of the material used in this book, whether companies or individuals. Any omission is unintentional, and we will be pleased to correct errors in future editions of this book.

Text acknowledgments:

p. 4: Philokalia. *Writings from the Philokalia.* E. E. Kadloubovsky and G. E. H. Palmer, trans. Faber, London, 1951.

pp. 23, 30, 32, 37, 52: Cohen, J. M. and J.-F. Phipps. *The Common Experience.* Rider & Co., London, 1979.

p. 31: Plotinus. *The Enneads.* S. Mc-Kenna, trans. Faber, London, 1956.

p. 33: Attar. *The Persian Mystics.* M. Smith, trans. John Murray, London, 1932.

p. 41: Bancroft, Anne. *The Luminous Vision: Six Medieval Mystics and their Teachings.* Allen & Unwin, London, 1982.

p. 42: Lull, Ramon. *The Book of the Lover and the Beloved.* E. Allison Peers, trans. Society for Promoting Christian Knowledge, London, 1946.

p. 47: *Meister Eckhart* (2 vols.). J. Evans, trans. Watkins, London, 1924.

p. 48: Suso, Henry. *The Little Book of Eternal Wisdom.* J. M. Clark, trans. Faber, London, 1953.

Picture acknowledgments:

Abtei St. Hildegarde; Pages: 5, 7, 13, 17, 19, 31, 37, 41, 46, 47, 59.
Scala Istituto Fotografico; Pages: 8, 24, 28, 38, 56, 57.
Bodleian Library; Pages: 14, 18, 27, 34.
Hodalic Arne; Pages: 20, 23, 42.
The Wallace Collection; Page: 25.
Spanish Tourist Office; Page: 50.
St. Joan's Int'l Alliance; Page 53.